Retirement Roots

A Christian Plan For Everyday Life In Retirement

By Robert S. Laura

Published by Retirement Project LLC

RetirementProject.org

Copyright 2014 Robert S. Laura
Adapted From Previous Works

Printed in the United States of America

ISBN 13: 978-0-9754250-8-4

Robert S. Laura. – 1st ed.

Retirement Roots

Cover Art by: Michael LaFountain 2014

Published by Retirement Project LLC Brighton MI
RetirementProject.org

RetirementBibleStudy.com

DEDICATION

This book would not be possible without God and the love and support of so many people who have helped me rediscover my faith and strengthen my relationship with Jesus Christ. Members of our Church, Bible Study, and Mastermind Group, as well and my best friend and amazing wife Amie and our beautiful children: Connor, Ava, Lucas, and Drake.

Words cannot express how I feel about the foundation, strength, and love you have all given me.

CONTENTS

INTRODUCTION

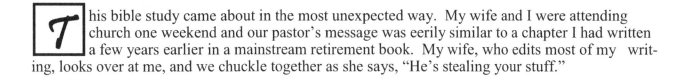

*T*his bible study came about in the most unexpected way. My wife and I were attending church one weekend and our pastor's message was eerily similar to a chapter I had written a few years earlier in a mainstream retirement book. My wife, who edits most of my writing, looks over at me, and we chuckle together as she says, "He's stealing your stuff."

The very next week, the same thing happened. A portion of the pastor's message was spot on to several points I had made in my book. So, we laugh again, this time as I lament, "He's not even giving me credit for the material he's stealing."

And I'm not joking, it happened the next week as well. For three straight weeks my pastor was blatantly using my work as his own. Well that's not completely true. His message to our church for those three weeks contained many of the same topics I had written about in my retirement book including the need to plan for the mental, social, physical, and spiritual aspects of life after work.

So, I came to realize that my pastor wasn't stealing or even borrowing my content, I was being nudged by the Holy Spirit to connect the dots; to bring a biblical perspective to traditional retirement and help people understand how Scripture can help people create a new, more personal narrative that is rooted in passion and purpose to glorify God.

I am grateful for the opportunity to share this work with you, but being completely transparent, it's not a job I wanted or felt qualified to do. I didn't want to become a Christian financial advisor and go around offering this book and workshop. Don't get me wrong, I love the Lord, my church and small group... but I was truly content with keeping my spiritual and professional life separate.

But that wasn't God's plan for me. It's interesting because I definitely tried to drag my feet with the whole thing. I guess I was hoping God might be interested in following my plan instead or that another assignment might come up if I waited long enough. Now, more than ever, I am grateful for trusting in Him and the opportunities this ministry has created for me.

Of course, that doesn't necessarily make it easy because as part of the process, I have to change everything you have ever been told or taught about retirement. For some of you, that may mean undoing twenty of thirty years of brainwashing or for others, it may mean 5-10 years. In any event, I know I have my work cut out for me, but I feel ready and prepared with more than 2,000 years of Bible wisdom, promises, and characters.

Retirement Roots was written to provide you with concrete steps and exercises to transform retirement planning from a numbers-based approach to a new method that injects joy and passion based on God's word.

INTRODUCTION

As you read through *Retirement Roots*, I hope you can envision retirement planning in a new way… one where God's promises and truth lead to a simpler, more peaceful retirement. Specifically, the workbook:

☑ Teaches you how to turn an earthly retirement into an everlasting one

☑ Prepares you to overcome Satan's temptations and the dark side of retirement

☑ Asks you the three most powerful retirement questions that can change your life forever

☑ Prepares you for important conversations about your transition that will strengthen your relation ships with God, family, and friends

☑ Helps you replace your work identity, fill your time and keep you connected by building both a retirement "Curious List" and a "Friend List."

☑ Provides ongoing results and points of reflection through a one-page, inspirational *Christian Retirement Plan*

Today's realities say it's time to focus more on God's saving grace than your personal savings. Use *Retirement Roots* to discover the best of what God has in store for you.

Chapter 1

RETIREMENT REALITY

"For I know the plans I have for you," declares the LORD, *"plans to prosper you and not to harm you, plans to give you hope and a future."*

Jeremiah 29:11 NIV

RETIREMENT REALITY

hat if I told you that the best place to learn about retirement is the Bible? What if the good book actually overflows with ideas, examples, and even characters that are just as relevant to life in retirement today as they were for the way people lived thousands of years ago.

For example, consider Abraham, who was called by God at age 75 to leave behind everything he knew for a new purpose in an unknown destination. He didn't have all the answers or know what was waiting for him on the other side. But he knew God had a plan for him and he followed that calling. So many people go into retirement planning with the goal of having it all figured out. But that's now how it works. You have to know that like Abraham, God wants you to rely on Him and look to Him for direction.

We can also use the story of Daniel for those people who may be considering retirement because of issues with their co-workers or threats of a company closing. Daniel was betrayed by his co-workers and thrown into the lion's den, which he survived thanks to his unwavering faith. Faith isn't often talked about in traditional retirement planning, but each and every person in retirement will inevitably face a number of their own lion dens.

In fact, there is something called the Homes Rahe scale that contains a list of the 43 most stressful life events. Situations that people go through that can make them physically sick or emotional scarred. Guess what the 10th most stressful life event is? Yes, it's retirement. Additionally, 20 of those 43 stress factors can show up near or in retirement. That makes having a strong relationship with God more important than ever during this transition.

Finally, there may be some people who are still a few years away or in the early stages of it who are thinking about going in a new direction such as switching careers, starting a business, or going back to school. In those instances, we can consider Paul, who was called to take his life in a direction that no one expected or anticipated, except of course, God.

In each case, the lives of Abraham, Daniel, and Paul all grew brighter as they pursued their faith and their relationship with God.

> *"After these things the word of the LORD came to Abram in a vision: "Fear not, Abram, I am your shield; your reward shall be very great." Genesis 15:1 ESV*

> *"So Daniel prospered during the reign of Darius and the reign of Cyrus the Persian." Daniel 6:28 NIV*

> *"I have been put up on the cross to die with Christ. I no longer live. Christ lives in me. The life I now live in this body, I live by putting my trust in the Son of God. He was the One Who loved me and gave Himself for me." Galatians 2:20 NIV*

RETIREMENT REALITY

In addition to talking about some of the Bible's popular characters, I also want to address the only reference to the concept of retirement in Scripture.

The word "*retire*" appears in every financial advisors' favorite book of the Bible, "*Numbers*." I'm kidding, but I do love God's sense of humor for putting it there because so many people attach the act of retirement to the dollars and cents of it, but as I have come to learn, God's approach to retirement has very little to do with money.

The specific verse is Numbers 8:23-26 and reads:

> "*The LORD said to Moses, [24] 'This applies to the Levites: Men twenty-five years old or more shall come to take part in the work at the tent of meeting, [25] but at the age of fifty, they must retire from their regular service and work no longer. [26] They may assist their brothers in performing their duties at the tent of meeting, but they themselves must not do the work. This, then, is how you are to assign the responsibilities of the Levites.'*"

As you can see, the verse essentially says, "Levites should retire at 50 and not do any work." Sounds good, right? Everyone retires at 50 and moves on to a life of leisure.

Well it's not that easy. The reality is, the Bible doesn't endorse the way many people perceive retirement. Nowhere does scripture offer ideas or suggestions for living a leisure filled, self-serving life. There's no extra commandments or prophet that says you can sit on the couch all day, let their relationships deteriorate, give up on their health and well-being, stop using their gifts and talents, and most of all, stop serving others.

That being said, you are not going to end up in hell because you accepted a buy-out offer or decided 35 years with the same company was enough. The challenge comes when people turn retirement into a self-centered phase of life rather than a God-centered one.

When this happens people can end up wasting years wandering around the deserts of retirement trying to figure it out on their own. Just as the Israelites wandered around in the wilderness for forty years to make what was an 21-28 day journey. The problem is, they don't go into retirement with a plan for the non-financial aspects of retirement. They don't have a plan to replace their work identity, fill their time, stay relevant and connected, as well as mentally and physically sharp.

In other words, they struggle to move on because they don't have a plan or vision for their everyday lives in retirement. They need to let go of the idea that they, and the money they have saved, will be enough to deal with the setbacks as well as the opportunities that will come along because the reality is, just as God has a plan for your retirement so too does the devil.

Live Longer

Travel
Traveling keeps your mind active through new places and cultural experiences, physically fit through walking and climbing stairs, and is a great way to meet new people and make new friends.

Friends
According to a study at Flinders University in Australia, people with an extensive networks of good friends and confidantes outlived those with the fewest friends by 22%.

Volunteer
According to a University of Michigan study, adults over 65 who volunteered at least 40 hours each year to a single cause were 40% more likely than non-volunteers to be alive at the end of study.

Prayer
According to the National Institutes of Health, people who pray daily are 40% less likely to have high blood pressure.

One where the bondage of addiction, the hollowness of depression, and even the fiery depths of suicide consume retirees who aren't armed and prepared for the battles ahead. Yes, there is a dark side to retirement which means that you need to be prepared to strap on the Armor of God in order to fight against it.

Another point I want to make is that retirement is often portrayed as life's ultimate goal and sign of freedom, but it's not. Getting into Heaven is. That's a powerful reality I don't want anyone to regret or realize too late. It's not like saying, "I sure wish I would have invested in gold when it was $800 an ounce" or "bought some shares of Apple when they first went public."

Managing financial regrets or other earthly issues during 20-30 years in retirement pales in comparison to where and how you will spend eternity. Having a relationship with God is a boat you (and those you love) don't want to miss.

As you will see, a Christian retirement is one that is founded in Biblical concepts instead of dollars and cents. It's about saving, building, and preparing for things that glorify God. Now don't get me wrong, there is still a need for individuals and couples to plan and save money for their retirement. After all, this book is not about asking you to quit your job, sell all your possessions, volunteer for every church committee, or give you a long list of *'Thou Shall Not's'*.

Instead, the goal is to help you see the God-given time you have set aside for retirement in a different perspective. One that is enjoyable and tunes you into the fact that your life and your legacy will ultimately be judged by God and not the details inside a binder full of financial charts and graphs.

The current way many people approach retirement planning needs to change dramatically because it's focused on the wrong things. That statement may come as a surprise since I'm a financial professional whose primary job is to make sure people understand how much they need to save, that they have the proper asset allocations, and to put strategies in place to ensure they don't run out of money.

Yet, I have found that each one of those planning factors mean very little compared to running out of family, close friends, good health, or a relationship with Jesus Christ.

The powerful reality here is that many people enter retirement with stress or concerns about how they will replace their work identity, fill their time with meaningful tasks, stay connected to family and friends, make their money last, and remain in good mental and physical health. The good news is that God is the ultimate tool and resource for retirement. For many it's just a matter of making a conscious shift to include Him in your plans. Something that is best exemplified by comparing your personal retirement voyage with two very popular, yet very different ships: Noah's Ark and The Titanic.

As you know, "professionals" built the Titanic and claimed it was unsinkable, while others mocked an amateur as he built the Ark. Without knowing the eventual result, the big, shinny ship may look like the perfect place to enjoy your retirement, but when you consider how both ended up, little doubt exists as to which ship and team I think you'd want to be on.

Noah and many other unlikely people throughout the Bible used God's word; His whisper to them to find and fulfill their purpose in life. Unfortunately, today, many people are just focused on the time and money they have on earth, and unknowingly preparing for a voyage on the Titanic: A journey that will never offer true happiness and joy just as the ship never settled into a port.

Inevitably, retirement without any God-given direction can be like the iceberg that sank the Titanic, where 90% of what you need to be thinking, saying, and doing stays below the surface and out of your traditional plan. Therefore, it's time to stop conforming to mainstream ideas and views about retirement and embrace God's word and the truth that comes with it.

Securing a Christian retirement today requires different tools and ammunition than it did in the past. It calls for new and soon-to-be retirees to invest first and foremost in their relationship with Christ. That means accepting the fact that for every hour invested in traditional retirement planning an equal amount of time should be spent in scripture and with your small group, pastor, or a trained advisor to help you plan for the mental, social, physical, and spiritual aspects of life in retirement.

What I know about retirement planning is that what we as individuals, and couples, choose to do and not do (what we write down and discuss and what we don't) can have a profound impact on the results we get. Therefore, I want to encourage you to make the most of your time, talents, and faith by completing each worksheet with what God has put on your heart and in your thoughts. It's an important step to aligning His wisdom and principles with your retirement.

This is important because many people assume that retirement is the end of their work years, just as Jewish leaders thought crucifying Jesus would end everything. But they couldn't have been more wrong as Christianity has flourished… and so can your life in retirement and beyond.

Are you ready to discover God's retirement plans for you?

Personal Reflections & Retirement Applications

How does Mathew 6:19-21 differ from that of mainstream retirement planning?

> *"Do not store up for yourselves treasures on earth, where moths and vermin destroy, and where thieves break in and steal. [20] But store up for yourselves treasures in heaven, where moths and vermin do not destroy, and where thieves do not break in and steal. [21] For where your treasure is, there your heart will be also." Matthew 6:19-21 NIV*

_____

_____

_____

_____

_____

_____

_____

What impact or influence does today's Church have on the concept of retirement?

_____

_____

_____

_____

_____

_____

_____

_____

Chapter 2

RETIREMENT PERCEPTIONS

"Trust in the LORD with all your heart,
and lean not on your own understanding"

Proverbs 3:5 NIV

RETIREMENT PERCEPTIONS

*O*ne of the biggest reasons people struggle to make a successful transition into retirement is because they rely on their own ability to understand and control it. Many pre-retirees create unrealistic expectations about how different and fulfilling it's going to be only to learn that on their own, their thoughts and desires don't exactly measure up. In fact, for many it doesn't even come close to what they hoped and mentally planned for it to be.

One researcher I spoke with stated that 75% of pre-retirees expect life in retirement to be better; but only 40% of actual retirees find that to be true. That's a major disconnect between perceptions and reality, and a fundamental reason why new and soon-to-be retirees need to open up their heart, mind, and eyes to the realities of everyday life in retirement.

Retirementality

"I think people's perception of a rich girl is literal, but metaphorically I embrace it as being rich in love, spirit, joy and religion. So it's not about money."

Angie Stone

"We know what we are, but not what we may be."

William Shakespeare

"The best way to find yourself is to lose yourself in the service of others."

Mahatma Ghandi

I can share with you that my own perceptions about retirement were shattered early in my career. A friend asked if I would help him and his son on a remodeling project. In between the sounds of a saw and hammer, I said to my buddy, "It must be great being retired… to have the time, money, and freedom to come and help out like this." He took a drink, looked me square in the eye, and said, "Bob, don't ever retire because, the minute you do, you won't mean anything to anyone, anymore." Those were his exact words, "You won't mean anything to anyone, anymore!"

That's an awfully harsh statement for a retiree to make, especially since retirement is supposed to be the Promised Land, where alarm clocks and busy schedules don't exist and you're only accountable for your golf score, or being on time for your spa treatment. There was an obvious disconnect between the freedom and joy retirement is supposed to provide and what he was actually experiencing.

Fact of the matter is, money and constant leisure have very little to do with true freedom which only God can provide. True freedom is void of fear, shame, guilt, and worry. It's knowing you're loved for who you are and loving others for what and where they are in life. It's an opportunity to genuinely be who you are and to live the life God created for you.

That makes it important for new and soon-to-be retirees to take the time to think about and begin to plan for what everyday life in retirement is really going to be like. To figure out, what it will take to be happy, fulfilled and among the 40% mentioned above who find life is better without a boss or daily commute.

Retirement Perception Quiz

On the next page is a fun and entertaining exercise that will challenge your perceptions about retirement relationships, work-identity, schedule, and physical wellbeing. Read the question and then circle one of the answer choices. Following the quiz, I'll explain the purpose behind each question and provide some scripture to help steer your perceptions toward what life in retirement can be, and is really like.

RETIREMENT PERCEPTIONS QUIZ

1. On your retirement cruise, you're left stranded on a deserted island. This is a big relief because you no longer have to deal with?

    a. Family member(s)
    b. Friend/relationship
    c. Money
    d. A specific commitment
    e. An impending decision you've been hesitant to make

2. A local organization is in desperate need of help. You're touched and call to offer one of the following items. Which one are you most likely to provide?

    a. Money, food and clothing
    b. Knowledge and other informational resources
    c. Personal skill
    d. Physical labor

3. To claim a $10,000 prize you must do one of the following. Which one would you avoid at all costs?

    a. Eat vegan for an entire year
    b. Run a half-marathon
    c. Step onto a scale, in your swimsuit, on national TV (like the show Biggest Loser)
    d. Reveal an unhealthy habit or behavior on Dr. Phil
    e. None of the above

4. A friend invites you to a party and upon arrival you realize your friend isn't there yet and you don't know a single soul. Do you?

    a. Scurry back to your car to wait for your friend
    b. Hide in a corner until your friend arrives
    c. Grab a plate and ask to sit with some strangers
    d. Seek out the host and introduce yourself

5. Some colleagues are talking about investments. Which would you suggest?

    a. High-yield dividend stocks, covered calls, and sector bets with ETFs
    b. They talk to your financial advisor
    c. Put half their money in CDs and the rest under their mattress
    d. Excuse yourself claiming a sudden need to use the restroom

6. Which one of the following is your biggest fear in retirement?

    a. Outliving your money
    b. Being ripped off
    c. Losing a loved one
    d. Losing your identity
    e. Health/healthcare
    f. Staying connected

Question1: Stress

This is a powerful question because it shatters the perception that life in retirement is totally carefree and easy. It quickly and concisely pinpoints a major area of stress you may be carrying into retirement. Many soon-to-be retirees assume that problems or issues will just go away once they retire, but that's never the case. In fact, things can actually get worse because you will have more time to dwell on your problem, and fewer distractions to take your attention away from it. Whether your answer pertains to a relationship, time commitment, or something financial, start resolving this issue now by giving your concerns to God instead of dragging them with you into retirement.

God doesn't want you to worry. He wants all of us to hand-over our worries and concerns to Him. A powerful blessing that when applied, creates space for more positive thoughts and feelings about retirement and a true sense of freedom.

> *"Can any one of you by worrying add a single hour to your life"*
> *Matthew 6:27 NIV*

Question 2: Time & Identity

Many people plan to use some form of volunteering to help replace their work identity and fill their time. However, many retirees go into it with only general assumptions about it and can find themselves frustrated or burnt out instead of joyfully serving.

One way to be more definitive as to how and where you want to spend your time is to ask yourself, "What disturbs you? What distresses your heart and causes you to think, 'I need to do something about that'? When Esther was told her uncle was mourning the Kings decree to kill all Jews, she was deeply disturbed and realized she had to do something about it. Facing the possibility of execution, she finally realized the very reason God placed her on the throne. Retirement offers you the same opportunity to live out your purpose. To be a resource and guiding light.

God has bestowed great skills, talents, and opportunities upon you. While our bodies will naturally weaken as we grow older, if you don't utilize what God has given you, you will lose it. Now that doesn't mean you have to maintain an 8-10 hour work schedule or jump at every opportunity to stay busy and useful. God wants you to enjoy retirement and only asks in return that you use your gifts to serve others, and when called upon, make the most of the position He has put you in.

> *"Remember, the man who plants only a few seeds will*
> *not have much grain to gather. The man who plants*
> *many seeds will have much grain to gather."*
> *2 Corinthians 9:6 NIV*

Retiring Single?

You're not alone. Single people are now 96 million strong and make up 43 percent of the adult population.

In fact, three of every four single people age 65 or older are women.

Active Community
Consider living in an active community that has an activities director, whose job is to engage residents with one another.

The more activities and events there are, the greater your opportunities for staying involved.

New Best Friend
Make insurance your best friend. Consider disability insurance to protect your lifestyle and ability to save for retirement while working.

Then long-term care insurance to help pay for home care if you need help with your daily living needs.

Question 3: Physical Health

When it comes to physical health and retirement, a common trap people fall into is that they believe they will automatically use the extra time and flexibility in their schedule to exercise more and eat healthier. But retirement doesn't come with any extra motivation, and, as the saying goes, first we make our habits and then our habits make us. Which is why its important to start taking care of your body right now and to acknowledge the short-comings you have in this area of life... and ask God for support. After all, your body is only a short-term loan that you must not only care for, but also account for. What will you say when you return it?

It's also just as important for you to maintain strong mental health. The Bible is not all about restrictions. God knows that laughter and fun are part of a successful life and retirement, so make sure you're plans include things that will keep a smile on your face so that others will be encouraged to ask about your happiness.

> *"A cheerful heart is good medicine, but a crushed spirit dries up the bones."*
> *Proverbs 17:22 NIV*

Question 4: Social Style

Many people don't take the time to stop and consider their social situation during retirement. They don't realize that they'll be around fewer people than when they were working. For some, that difference is easily overcome; but it may be more difficult for others. Furthermore, we are called to belong, not just believe. God made this obvious early on when in the Garden of Eden He said, "It is not good for the man to be alone." (Genesis 2:18 NIV). We are created for community and none of us can fulfill God's purposes by ourselves.

Therefore, as you approach retirement, make sure you are investing in others and cultivating relationships outside of the workplace. Fellowship or being part of a group and building new relationships are proven methods of increasing longevity and play an important role in fending off conditions such as depression.

> *"Two people are better off than one, for they can help each other succeed.*
> *[10] If one person falls, the other can reach out and help. But someone who falls alone is in real trouble. [11] Likewise, two people lying close together can keep each other warm. But how can one be warm alone?*
> *[12] A person standing alone can be attacked and defeated, but two can stand back-to-back and conquer. Three are even better, for a triple-braided cord is not easily broken."*
> *Ecclesiastes 4:9-12 NLT*

Question 5: Money

While there won't be much about financial matters in this book, people today are more responsible for their retirement savings than ever before, and shouldn't assume every investment or advisor is right for them (even if they go to the same church or are labeled as 'faith-based'). That means it's essential that individuals and couples are able to articulate the basics of money management and know at least some of the key questions to ask financial professionals in order to protect themselves against fraud, bad advice, or an investment scam. Whether you're investing in a new business or the stock market, use Gods wisdom and principles to guide you.

> *"Whoever loves money never has enough; whoever loves wealth is never satisfied with their income. This too is meaningless."*
> Ecclesiastes 5:10 NIV

Question 6: Retirement Concerns

So much retirement talk today is fear based. People are constantly bombarded with the idea that they are going to run out of money, be left alone, or suffer a debilitating medical condition. Which is why it's important to involve God and stop worshiping what-if's and other problems. You will inevitably face challenges throughout retirement, but often times, those situations are tests of your faith and an opportunity to grow closer to God. Therefore, face your fears with God for any delay will only slow your progress toward true freedom.

> *"Cast all your anxiety on him because he cares for you."*
> 1 Peter 5:7 NIV

Overall, your quiz answers represent the first step in helping you examine retirement in a more personal and less material way. One that is definitely different from the typical dollars-and-cents approach practiced by many.

The goal of this first exercise is to raise your awareness about not only the way you think and feel about retirement, but also the way in which a relationship and commitment to God can help. Doing so, will allow you to begin to resolve areas of stress and fear as well as make the most of the talent and opportunities God has offered you.

While this quiz is simple in nature, it's a prelude to a deeper, darker side of retirement that can affect those who don't have a plan to manage the mental, social, physical, and spiritual parts of it. Potential repercussions that can become major problems, temptations, or sources of conflict if they aren't addressed and planned for.

Retirementality

"The value of a man should be seen in what he gives and not in what he is able to receive."

Albert Einstein

"The best thing about the future is that it comes one day at a time."

Abraham Lincoln

Personal Reflections & Retirement Applications

_____
_____
_____
_____
_____
_____
_____
_____
_____
_____
_____
_____
_____
_____
_____
_____
_____
_____
_____
_____
_____
_____
_____
_____
_____
_____
_____
_____

Chapter 3

DARK SIDE OF RETIREMENT

"One day the angels came to present themselves before the LORD, and Satan also came with them. [7] The LORD said to Satan, 'Where have you come from?' Satan answered the LORD, 'From roaming throughout the earth, going back and forth on it.'"

Job 1:6-7

DARK SIDE OF RETIREMENT

R etirement is often depicted as an idyllic life of leisure filled with contentment and joy. You might envision long walks on the beach, worldwide travel, quality time with family, or turning your memoirs into a NY Times bestseller, but retirement is just like every other phase of life. It can come with a dark side that's seldom discussed, and rarely planned for.

Unfortunately, just as God has a plan for your retirement so too does the devil. One where the bondage of addiction, the hollowness of depression, and even the fiery depths of suicide consume retirees who aren't armed and prepared for the battles ahead.

This topic came about after a casual conversation with a local doctor. After I outlined the premise of this book I asked him if there was anything he observed in retired patients that I might be missing. "One of the biggest issues with retirees," he said, "is addiction." Surprised, I asked him for more details and felt compelled to begin my own research.

I can tell you that I was stunned by what I discovered. There is a hidden epidemic taking place in the shadows of retirement that highlight the pressing need for individuals and families to involve God in their retirement plans and prepare for much more than just the financial aspects of retirement.

Retirementality

"Be alert and of sober mind. Your enemy the devil prowls around like a roaring lion looking for someone to devour. Resist him, standing firm in the faith, because you know that the family of believers throughout the world is undergoing the same kind of sufferings."

1 Peter 5:8-9 NIV

"Don't be drunk with wine, because that will ruin your life. Instead, be filled with the Holy Spirit,"

Ephesians 5:18 NLT

"God is our refuge and strength, an ever-present help in trouble."

Psalm 46:1 NIV

A Chilling Prescription

It is expected that by 2020, the number of retirees with alcohol and other drug problems will leap 150% to 4.4 million – up from 1.7 million in 2001.

According to the Substance Abuse and Mental Health Services Administration, the proportion of older people treated for a combination of cocaine and alcohol abuse tripled between 1992 and 2008. For this group, in 2008, cocaine abuse was the leading cause of admissions involving drugs (26.2%), with abuse of prescription drugs a close second at 25.8%.

An Emotional Recession

The National Institutes of Health report that, of the 35 million Americans age 65 or older, about two million suffer from full-blown depression. Another five million suffer from less severe forms of the illness.

Women are at a greater risk for depression because of biological factors such as hormonal changes and the stress that comes with maintaining relationships or caring for loved ones or children who are ill.

Health conditions, including heart attack, stroke, hip fracture or macular degeneration, and procedures such as bypass surgery, can also trigger the onset of depression.

Depression is also the single most significant risk factor for suicide among the elderly. Sadly, many of those who commit suicide did, in fact, reach out for help – 20% see a doctor on the day they die, 40% the same week and 70% the same month.

DARK SIDE OF RETIREMENT

The Ultimate Crash

Suicide is the 11th leading cause of death in the United States, with an aggregate rate of 11 suicide deaths per 100,000 Americans. Suicide rates are highest among people over the age of 65, according to the American Association of Suicidology (AAS). That age group makes up 12.5% of the population and accounts for 15.9% of all suicides.

White men older than age 65 take their own life at almost triple the overall rate, and are eight times more likely to commit suicide than women in the same age group. Perhaps surprisingly, white men age 85 and older have the highest annual suicide rate of any group — 51.4 deaths per 100,000. In contrast, the rate among white women peaks between ages 45 and 64 at 7.8 deaths per 100,000.

As surprising as this information may seem, the threat of addiction, depression, and suicide becomes even more real as you examine their contributing factors. For example, baby boomers were the first generation to engage in the widespread use of recreational drugs, and the first group for which a wide variety of prescription medications were readily available and culturally accepted as treatment for nearly every ailment. They are also now at a critical stage in life where stress can mount due to natural aging, bodily dysfunction, grief and loss, plus the financial strain that often stems from caring for both aging parent(s) and adult children/grandchildren.

This shadowy downside of retirement appears to be exacerbated by the fact that today's seniors are from a generation that stressed self-reliance: A trait characterized by a reluctance to discuss financial and/or personal health matters. This attribute, reinforced by scientific research, suggests that contemporary seniors tend to blame themselves for their illnesses, don't want to be a burden on family, and worry that treatment will be too costly. Further evidence that much of what really takes place in retirement lies below the surface and out of mainstream conversations and retirement planning.

The remainder of the book will continue to help you explore ways in which you can use Gods word and power in defeating the dark side of retirement and also adding purpose, meaning, and joy to the ever day things you do in the next phase of your life.

Saving Grace Account

Most financial experts preach the importance of having a rainy day fund equal to 3-6 months of expenses to cover emergencies or unexpected costs. The same concept should be applied to your personal life in retirement. A Saving Grace Account cushions you when a challenge such as the loss of a loved one, financial hardship, an unforeseen medical diagnosis, or difficult decision leaves you vulnerable to Satan's ways and temptation.

Joseph And The Well

In Genesis 50:20, Joseph is speaking to his brothers, who had severely mistreated him. When they threw him down a well and sold him into slavery, they thought they were working against him, but God had a different plan.: One that was much bigger and that would use those trials to make him a powerful influencer.

Sometimes the very things we think are awful turn out to be a great blessing and time to develop our faith.

You may find yourself in a deep well from time to time, but God has a plan to use that place. Person or situation to promote you in His Kingdom, God knows all, and He will use those trials and tribulations for your good.

"Even when I walk through the darkest valley, I will not be afraid, for you are close beside me."

Psalm 23:4 NLT

DARK SIDE OF RETIREMENT

This support network can be just as important, if not more important, than a financial savings account.

In times of trouble we need to be able to turn to God and others to bring light into our dark world. Create a Saving Grace Account by listing your family, friends, professionals and organizations that you can request prayers from as well as rely upon for help and support during emergencies and unexpected life events.

- Who do you turn to when times get tough or you're faced with a difficult situation?

- Who gets the first phone call when you're feeling down and need a pick me up?

- Who provides wise counsel or time-tested advice?

- Who can and will pray for you?

- Who has been there in the past when you needed help, a hug, or wake up call?

- Who can you ask for financial support?

- Who would help you move into a retirement community, or nurse you back to health after a knee or hip replacement?

_____   _____

_____   _____

_____   _____

_____   _____

_____   _____

Whether its addiction, depression, gambling, suicide, a difficult time or life-changing medical diagnosis, don't worship the problem. Rejoice in the Lord and seek his help first and above all else.

> *"For we are not fighting against flesh-and-blood enemies, but against evil*
> *rulers and authorities of the unseen world, against mighty powers in this*
> *dark world, and against evil spirits in the heavenly places."*
> *Ephesians 6:12 NLT*

Personal Reflections & Retirement Applications

What are some ways that Satan can work against your retirement plans?

_____

_____

_____

_____

What temptations pose the greatest threat to your retirement plans and goals?

_____

_____

_____

_____

Describe a difficult time in your life. How did you deal with it, who did you turn to, and what did you learn from it?

_____

_____

_____

_____

"Even though I walk through the darkest valley, I will fear no evil, for you are with me;
your rod and your staff, they comfort me." Psalm 23:4 NIV

"Blessed is the one who perseveres under trial because, having stood the test, that person will
receive the crown of life that the Lord has promised to those who love him." James 1:12 NIV

"And we know that in all things God works for the good of those who love him,
who have been called according to his purpose." Romans 8:28 NIV

Chapter 4

RETIREMENT FOUNDATIONS

*"Let your roots grow down into him, and let your lives be built on him.
Then your faith will grow strong in the truth you were taught,
and you will overflow with thankfulness."*

Colossians 2:7 NLT

RETIREMENT FOUNDATIONS

*T*raditional retirement planning typically includes a "visioning" or goal-based discussion that usually revolves around big picture items that require savings. For example, annual travel, a second home, or maintaining a lifestyle based on a percentage of your pre-retirement income.

What's missing are the intangibles; the thoughts, feelings, and experiences that are at the root of living a fulfilling and meaningful retirement. In order to assemble the missing pieces it's important to figure out how your faith and relationship with God fit into it, as well as what's truly important about your time during it.

My own epiphany regarding retirement came when I had the opportunity to meet with my first millionaire client. As you can imagine I was excited for the meeting because I was certain it would reveal some enlightening information that would set me on my own path to riches. During the course of our conversation, I was finally able to ask the million dollar question, "What was the best investment you ever made?"

Of course I went into the meeting wondering if she just got lucky in real estate, somehow knew Sam Walton, or had kids with ties to Microsoft and Bill Gates. Which is why I was shocked and extremely disappointed when, without hesitation, she said that the best investment she ever made was, "the Craft-matic Adjustable Bed."

Retirementality

"No one can serve two masters. Either you will hate the one and love the other, or you will be devoted to the one and despise the other. You cannot serve both God and money."

Mathew 6:24 NIV

"What good is it for a man to gain the whole world, yet forfeit his soul?"

Mark 8:36 NIV

Well, that brought me back down to earth in a hurry. I thought I was going to somehow get rich as a result of this meeting but here I was walking away with nothing more than a product testimonial from a late-night infomercial. I wanted to ask her if she owned the "Clapper," too, since they seem like they would go together.

At the time, I was serving the wrong master and was so focused on money, I didn't much care that her Craft-matic gave her a great night sleep. Yet, what I didn't know then, but do now, is that life, at any stage, isn't defined by money, investments, or a net worth, but rather by God and the Craft-matics He puts into your life that keep you happy and fulfilled. And that's exactly what we are going to uncover next with our Retirement Foundations questions and worksheet.

Answer the following questions in as much detail, and with as much feeling and conviction, as possible. This exercise can have a powerful impact on your retirement if you put effort into your answers, and allow what they reveal to work for you.

Spend as much time as you need on each question before moving onto the next section.

RETIREMENT FOUNDATIONS

1 What's your absolutely perfect retirement? How much money would you love to have saved? How much income will you live on each year? Will you travel? Serve on a mission trip or start your own ministry? Live in more than one location? What hobbies and leisure activities will you participate in? What will you do with your time? What hopes and dreams have been on hold until retirement? Below, be specific about what your perfect day and perfect week will look like.

Perfect Retirement

_____

_____

_____

_____

_____

Perfect Day In Retirement

Morning:

_____

_____

Afternoon:

_____

_____

Evening:

_____

_____

Perfect Week In Retirement

Sunday: _____

Monday: _____

Tuesday: _____

Wednesday: _____

Thursday: _____

Friday: _____

Saturday: _____

2 Imagine that the day after you retire your doctor informs you that you have only five years to live. Stop for a moment and let the emotional impact set in. Your life has just been cut short by 20-30 years, and your ideal retirement has just vanished. Think about how your life will change knowing that your ability to experience and enjoy it will be gone in five short years. Now, what will your focus in retirement be? Describe what you would want to accomplish, see, or do during your final years.

RETIREMENT FOUNDATIONS

3 Suppose you went back to your doctor and were suddenly informed that you have just 24 hours to live. Instead of concentrating on what you would do with your remaining time, ask yourself, what regrets would you have? What hopes and dreams would go unfulfilled? What do you wish you had accomplished, seen, felt, and experienced in your life now that it is at its end? How will you be remembered? What will your legacy be? What account of your life will you provide to God?

_____

_____

_____

_____

_____

_____

_____

_____

_____

_____

_____

_____

_____

_____

_____

_____

_____

_____

_____

_____

_____

_____

_____

_____

_____

_____

_____

_____

_____

_____

_____

_____

Take a minute to think about your answers to these questions and what they brought to light for you. What did you come to understand about yourself and what's important to you in retirement? Did your idea of a perfect retirement in Section 1 differ from what you identified as the most essential in Section 3?

This exercise represents the next step in changing your retirement from average to everlasting. Often, when people are asked to define their perfect retirement, their answers are based on things society values and we use to compare and judge each other - a practice that can limit one's personal dreams and Gods plan for you. Typically, money, possessions, hobbies and things of this nature dominate this area.

But when you focus on the things that are important and effect your eternal resting place, the results change from what others value to thoughts, actions, and plans that align you with Gods values. Ironically, the savings you need for retirement, as well as any anxiety you have about it, tend to decrease as you shift your focus from what you *think* would make it perfect to relying on what *will* make it everlasting.

This point is highlighted in an interview I had with Pastor Rick Warren, author of the extremely popular and best-selling book, *A Purpose Driven Life*. He shared with me, "As a pastor, I have stood at the bedside of literally thousands of people as they took their last breath. I have never once had somebody at their dying moment say, 'Bring me my bowling trophy, I want to see it one more time; bring me my degree, so I can look at it one more time; bring me the nice gold watch I got for 30 years of service at my company.' Nobody ever says that. They say, 'Bring me the people that I love.' In the closing moments of their life, what people want are those they love the most around them. We all eventually figure out that life is all about love. I just hope people learn that sooner."

> ## *Before You Retire*
>
> *When you retire it seems the data bank of all the things you didn't have time to do while working goes blank. It's a rite of passage that can leave many people wondering how best to spend their time. Therefore, don't rely on remembering all of those things. Instead, commit to getting yourself a pocket size notebook where you can write down all the things you don't have time to do, want to do, and need to do.*
>
> *This way you'll not only fill your days with things that mean the most to you, you'll also avoid common retirement traps like boredom.*

Pastor Warren's advice and this exercise also bring one of the major flaws of traditional retirement planning into focus. The idea that you have 20-30 years to do whatever you want with…. to accomplish all the things you expect to get done or experience on your own terms and timeline. Rest assured, however, that's not always the case. The hard reality is, things can change very quickly in retirement, and the only earthly guarantee that comes with it, is that at some point, you will die.

I recently had a client share with me that he was diagnosed with prostate cancer and was receiving radiation treatment for it. That was the good news. In the same month that his wife retired she was also diagnosed with lung cancer and given six months to live. That's a game changer. As you can imagine, retirement for them has taken on a completely different look and feel than they ever envisioned.

Similarly, there was the case of the chief of police and his wife of 50 years. They had a story book retirement complete with selling their house at a major premium just before the real estate market collapsed in 2007. They loved to golf, dance, and entertain until she suffered a stroke.

RETIREMENT FOUNDATIONS

A colossal change that dramatically altered their plans and life in retirement. Most people would agree that doesn't seem fair but, sadly, it happens all the time. These personal situations, and others like them, bring to light a common misconception of some Christians: That our lives should be perfect simply because we are Christ followers. But Jesus clearly warned us that trials and tribulations are a part of life.

> *"I have told you all this so that you may have peace in me. Here on earth you will have many trials and sorrows. But take heart, because I have over come the world." John 16:33 NLT*

Frankly, questions about our own mortality or ability to enjoy retirement seem like the ideal conversations to avoid … and most people do. But one of God greatest gifts is choice and I am asking you to choose differently by doing the exact opposite. Instead, use those conversations as motivating factors. Never assume you have unlimited time in retirement to just do whatever you want, whenever you can, because you may never get the chance.

Give your retirement more meaning by approaching it as if every day could be your last. Get your arms around the essential things, such as spending time with family and friends, serving others, and rooting yourself in God's word and truths.

Take a minute, now, to go back and update what your perfect day and week will look like. Then use that updated page to create a No-Regrets Retirement Plan. For those of you who really let the emotional impact set in and drive your answers, I can assure you that you're transforming your retirement into a blessing which only God can provide!

Personal Reflections & Retirement Applications

_____
_____
_____
_____
_____
_____
_____
_____
_____
_____
_____
_____
_____
_____
_____
_____
_____
_____
_____
_____
_____
_____
_____

Chapter 5

RETIREMENT CURIOUS & FRIEND LISTS

"There is no greater love than to lay down one's life for one's friends."

John 15:13 NLT

RETIREMENT CURIOUS & FRIEND LISTS

*T*wo of the biggest issues facing new retirees are 1) what to do with their time and 2) how to leave their career identity behind and re-invent themselves. These two major retirement issues are generally disregarded by traditional retirement planning and contribute significantly to the stress and anxiety many people feel once they retire.

Replacing one's work identity can be particularly difficult. It's an issue because many people confuse who they are with what they do. They love their work and what it provides them in terms of structure, prestige, and focus; but they realize too late that their work can't love them back. A sudden inability to equate what you do with who you are can cause some retirees to lose their sense of purpose and stability. Put another way, it can make you feel lost, bored, and even brokenhearted - a short list of things you don't want retirement to include.

Retirementality

"We keep moving forward, opening new doors, and doing new things, because we're curious and curiosity keeps leading us down new paths."

Walt Disney

"Life must be lived and curiosity kept alive. One must never, for whatever reason, turn his back on life."

Eleanor Roosevelt

Fear and distress can overtake your life as you're forced to start over and redefine your life's plan and direction. Like the Israelites in the wilderness, many retirees can wander aimlessly for years until they get in agreement with God and let him define their purpose in retirement.

Once an executive was offered an early buyout that would put him into retirement a couple years earlier than expected. The buyout offer was so lucrative, he had to take it or risk losing major increases to his pension and severance pay. With retirement thrust on him earlier than expected, he began to miss his old work life. In an attempt to save his sanity, his wife encouraged him to find a place to volunteer so he signed on with a local charity, ringing a bell in front of a store during the winter holiday season.

During his first shift, a former business acquaintance noticed him and pointedly asked him, "John what are you doing?" The comment struck him as if this charity work was beneath him, and he shouldn't be doing it. When he was asked again, "What are you doing?" John froze and didn't have an answer.

He hadn't yet come to terms with the fact that he no longer ran a million-dollar division, and that his day was no longer filled with the things he did before. The prestige that came with an expensive suit and tie was gone. He didn't know who he was now that his corporate life was over. For the first time, no one could tell if he was a wealthy, high-profile decision maker or just a local drunk driver performing mandatory community service. The lesson is, that as long as you let your work define you and rely on what others think and say, the more difficult and empty retirement will be.

Fact is, major life changes like retirement are an open door for the devil to do his work. Satan loves to use change to disrupt your life. He wants you to focus on the negative aspects and everything that retirement is not. That's why it's important to continually refocus your retirement lens on God and His ultimate judgment, not individual assumptions or conclusions.

Curious List

To help address this identity replacement issue, and fill some newfound time, new and existing retirees should develop a "curious list." A curious list is exactly what it sounds like, a list of things you are interested in and, at some point during retirement, would like to consider learning more about.

RETIREMENT CURIOUS & FRIEND LISTS

What makes the curious list different from a "bucket list" or "honey-do list" is the fact that it does not require a specific commitment of time or energy. Instead, it simply denotes that you wish to spend some amount of time and energy at some point in the future exploring a particular subject. For example, you could be curious about sky diving, but that doesn't mean you have to do it. You could simply read a book about it, watch a documentary on it, or talk one of your friends into doing it.

The secret of the curious list lies in the fact that it creates a desire to do more, be more, or learn more. When you are curious about something you want to take that next step and see what's around the corner. Through small and simple steps you'll not only help build momentum in areas of interest but also gain useful insights, foster experience, and ultimately add energy and direction to your new life. All crucial elements to cultivating a new identity and filling your time with meaningful tasks.

With the worksheet at the end of the chapter, take five minutes to write down as many things as possible that you are curious about. If you have a hard time getting started, or get stuck, there is a list of examples at the bottom of the page that should trigger some responses. Think quietly for a moment, "What do I want to see, do, or be a part of?"

A good curious list will support a balanced retirement that incorporates mental and physical health, social activities, financial well-being, and spiritual growth. It will also go a long way in helping new and soon-to-be retires avoid any regrets about their decision to retire.

Friend List

We need human connections for physical, emotional, and spiritual health. God wants us to connect with others on an intimate level and grow together but most pre-retirees don't realize that once they are retired, the luxury of running into and connecting with people they know will suddenly and dramatically change. Research suggests that while working you may have up to 22 high quality (face-to-face) interactions with people on a daily basis.

When people retire, that number can get cut in half, to 11, and those interactions are generally of lesser quality because they are more likely to be by phone or email rather than face-to-face. That's a change many people aren't prepared for and one that can leave them feeling isolated and out-of-the-loop.

Fact is, many adults have not taken the time to look at who they surround themselves with or the impact others can have on their happiness in retirement. We all have that Debbie Downer friend who, as soon as you ask, *"How are things going?"* launches into a 15 minute tirade about how terrible life and the world are. How many times have you hoped for a heavenly intervention such as a bad connection or knock on the door to avoid their negativity?

---

2 Things To Do Before You Retire

Eat A Great Meal
Whether its lobster, filet mignon, or some other delicacy, make it an annual tradition to eat a meal that's good enough to be your last. Stimulate your taste buds in a way you'll never forget as you celebrate the finer things in life.

Take More Pictures
Those who stay socially engaged with others and who have a strong network of friends tend to live longer.

Therefore, one simple ways to connect with old and new friends is through pictures. Simply ask for their email or Facebook I.D. and offer to send them copies of photos or tag them in it.

It's a proven way o create lasting memories as well as new relationships.

Retirement Roots

Get Creative

A couple planned to travel extensively in retirement. She retired from a major airline while he walked away from an automotive company.

So what was their creative retirement travel plan?

Her former employer offered retirees lifetime airfare for $50. She took a part-time job for a hotel chain, while he secured a part-time gig with a rental car agency.

Both provided deep discounts to employees in all of their favorite travel hot spots.

This represents a forward thinking approach that creates income, discounts, and most of all, the ability to achieve their retirement dreams.

"Where there is no vision, the people perish:"

Proverbs 29:18

Reality is, as Christians we have a responsibility to be the light to others but we can't be responsible for someone else's happiness. The only solution to anyone's earthly problems is through Jesus Christ. Without God as a filter, it's easy to get caught up in the wrong situations and thinking, which can have a profound impact on your mood and attitude.

On the other hand, we all have that friend who constantly has a smile, a kind word, or lending hand. So, as you transition into retirement, it's important to think about who you are going to surround yourself with, and how those people will affect you.

One Harvard study suggests that your odds of being happy increase by 15% if a direct connection in your network of friends is also happy. Even indirect connections, like having a happy friend of a friend, can increase your chances of being happy by as much as 10%. That may not seem like a big increase but the same study also reveals that an increase in annual income of approximately $10,000 was associated with just a 2% increase in the likelihood of being happy.

With this in mind, take five minutes to write down as many happy, vibrant, and energizing people you know. Think about people you like being around, who always have a smile on their face, who like to laugh, and share a mutual interest with you. Contemplate, who would you lay your life down for and vice versa? With whom can your faith grow?

Finally, when you're done, take a couple minutes to connect the people on your friends list with items on your curious list. Draw a line between the two groups where there may be a link, desire, or opportunity for a shared experience or interest with a friend. Try to build an eventual list of at least 15-20 curious items with 10 or more family members and friends with whom you see opportunities to explore new experiences.

This is an important exercise because it identifies who you want in your circle of influence, who you want to grow and learn with, who will pick you up when you're down, and who you can count on to help you stay connected.

Don't just put a name on the list and assume they, in turn, know how you feel about them. Make a commitment today to not only reach out and solidify your retirement plans with them but also with God. Let both know what their relationship means to you. The benefits are endless!

Regardless of whether you call them, email them, or send them a Facebook message, commit to taking the first steps now to strengthen those relationships. No one will be upset over receiving a message that says "you're a good friend and I want you to know you're someone I appreciate and want to continue our friendship well into retirement."

Retirement Roots

Introspective View

On the surface, it seems easy to assess other people's friendships, moods and attitudes, which is why it's important to examine your own as well. We all need people in our lives who will be caring, supportive, candid, reliable and committed. But there is only one way you're going to get people like this in your life: You have to be that kind of friend first. Ask yourself, "Would somebody put me on their friends list?" Would they invite you to experience something on their curious list? Why or why not? Take a moment to think about what makes for a good friendship: Consider things like reaching out to them on a regular basis, sharing with them what's going in in your life, and investing time and energy into things they care about and enjoy. Think about how you can do this with and for God.

"And let us consider how we may spur one another on toward love and good deeds"
Hebrews 10:20 NIV

Together, the curious and friendship lists provide a key for unlocking barriers to replacing your work identity, filling your time with more meaningful things, and staying connected to happy, energetic people. It's a powerful combination that will move you another step closer to God and a rewarding retirement.

RETIREMENT CURIOUS & FRIEND LISTS

Curious List	Friend List
1) _____	_____
2) _____	_____
3) _____	_____
4) _____	_____
5) _____	_____
6) _____	_____
7) _____	_____
8) _____	_____
9) _____	_____
10) _____	_____
11) _____	_____
12) _____	_____
13) _____	_____
14) _____	_____
15) _____	_____

Curious List Examples:

Writing a book	Religion/The Bible	Scuba diving
Skydiving	Your grandchildren	Family tree
Painting	Theatre	Choir
Musical instrument	Second language	Foreign culture
Song writing	Horseback riding	Sailing
Sign language	Special needs children	Dancing
Economics	Computers	Card games
Safari	Hot air balloons	Classic cars
Antiques	Foreign country	Gardening
Sporting events/teams	Museums	Airplanes
Magic	Whale watching	Cold case files

Personal Reflections & Retirement Applications

Retirement Roots

_____
_____
_____
_____
_____
_____
_____
_____
_____
_____
_____
_____
_____
_____
_____
_____
_____
_____
_____
_____
_____
_____
_____
_____

Chapter 6

RETIREMENT WELL-BEING

"Do you not know that you are God's temple and that God's Spirit dwells in you? [17] If anyone destroys God's temple, God will destroy him. For God's temple is holy, and you are that temple."

1 Corinthians 3:16-17 ESV

A good deal of our ability to prosper in our retirement years is dependent on keeping our bodies, mind and spirit healthy. Many retirees may be prepared for the financial aspects of their golden years, but they don't have an exercise routine, nutritional guidelines, or strategies to avoid boredom, bad habits, or losing one or more of their five senses. People are living longer nowadays, but that doesn't necessarily mean they will remain active and inspired during those additional years… and all the freedom and money in the world won't change that.

Retirementality

"There is nothing that wastes the body like worry, and one who has any faith in God should be ashamed to worry about anything whatsoever."

Mahatma Gandhi

"It takes more than just a good looking body. You've got to have the heart and soul to go with it."

Epictetus

"A cheerful heart is good medicine, but a crushed spirit dries up the bones."

Proverbs 17:22 NIV

In fact, most people don't realize that retirement only magnifies what you already are, particularly when it comes to health. If you frequent the couch, prefer fatty foods, or are always trying to please others, retirement will only provide more time to reinforce those habits.

That's why it's important to take as much care of your health as you do your wealth, because the best legacy you can give your family is a faithful and healthy you.

Therefore, in addition to knowing how much you need to save, how your assets should be allocated, and how much you can withdraw each year, make sure you consistently monitor numbers like these as well:

- Cholesterol level
- Fasting blood sugar level
- Body mass index (BMI)
- Blood pressure
- Resting heart rate

Measures of health like these are important because when God calls on you, He wants you to be ready, willing, and able to meet that call. It's easy to let exercise and eating habits slip, and I'm not suggesting that retirees don't deserve some down time after working for 30 or 40 years, but God doesn't want you to be lazy and retire from taking care of the body He gave you.

In Biblical times, they didn't have to worry about getting enough exercise or squeezing in a visit to the gym. They walked everywhere and had physically demanding jobs. But most of us today have sedentary jobs and need to develop a regular exercise plan that will make the most of what God has entrusted to us.

I think it's also important to note that taking control of your health in retirement doesn't mean you have to spend hours in the gym and sweat your way back to how you looked at 25. Nor does it mean that you have to rely on your own will power, starve yourself, or use surgery to alter your appearance. Just as we are redefining your thoughts and ideas about retirement, a similar change is necessary when it comes to getting healthy in retirement. Don't rely on your own knowledge or past experiences. Seek out the gifts and skills of local fitness professionals and culinary experts that will keep you functional and fun, not famished and weary.

RETIREMENT WELL-BEING

Therefore, as you develop new plans and activities to address this area of retirement health, lean on God's favor to direct and guide you to the right people and places. Don't try and turn back the clock in the first week or two. Be patient because there are no overnight crops. Literally, find ways through books and music to walk with the Lord when you exercise, cook, and eat.

Retirement health is not only about your physical health and what you're eating, but also what might be eating you? If your body and soul are filled with fear, resentment, worry, guilt, anger or other emotional issues, it will show up in your physical appearance and your behavior.

Emotional health requires that you have time to yourself and the space in your life to adapt to what's happening. Being overwhelmed or stressed out can leave you feeling inadequate and easy to anger around your loved ones. Furthermore, when God steps into your life, you should be ready and able, not bothered by another thing to put on your to do list. Therefore, just as you would sign up for an exercise class or set a regular workout schedule, set time aside everyday to get in agreement with God and to rest your mind.

In addition to helping you create a health plan to keep your body and mind strong, in motion, and protected against common disease, I also want to make you more aware of health factors that aren't often talked about, like losing one of your five senses such as vision or hearing.

I recently learned that a client had to surrender her driver's license. At just 67, her optometrist was unable to provide the script she needed to get her license renewed because of her declining peripheral vision. A bitter pill to swallow for a single woman living on the outskirts of town with few family and friends close by to drive her around. With only a local shuttle service available, a simple trip to the grocery store now takes her over 5 hours.

> ## Goals To Help You Get Ready For Retirement
>
> *Commit to meeting and making at least one new friend before you retire.*
>
> *Sign up for a new exercise class or find an active club that hikes, bikes, or mall walks.*
>
> *Give yourself a weekend away with a book and music to help you count your blessing and prepare for the next phase of life.*
>
> *Practice saying "No" to people and things you can't take on or that are emotionally draining.*

No one goes into retirement dreaming of a five hour bus trip just to buy a few groceries, or being dependent on family and friends to ferry them around. Similarly, another client said he had over fifty family members and friends at his house over the holidays. You might consider that a blessing but he complained bitterly that his hearing has declined to such an extent he can no longer participate in group discussions. Thus, he felt isolated and out of touch in his own home even though he was surrounded by people he loves and who love him.

On the surface, these situations may seem disheartening but you have to be prepared to adjust your life in retirement to God's direction. He may simply be asking you to focus on a few important relationships instead of many or that it's time to move closer to town for things you need.

Whether it's the loss of an important sense, your physical body, or mental capacity, the best strategy to combat their decline is to maintain a healthy, active lifestyle. Use the Retirement Well-Being section on the next page to highlight 1) healthy habits you'd like to start or continue 2) health opportunities such as things you want to see, hear, and do on your own or as part of a group; and 3) health concerns which can include aspects of your family health history that you should begin to address.

RETIREMENT WELL-BEING

#1 Healthy Habits: Identify three health-related *habits* you plan to continue or start in retirement. For example: walking, biking, swimming, taking vitamins, meditating on God's word, eating vegetarian, eliminating gluten from your diet, eating more fruits and vegetables, cooking a healthy meal once a week, etc.

1) _____

2) _____

3) _____

#2 Health Opportunities: Identify three health-related *opportunities* that you plan to take advantage of in retirement, including things you may want to see, speak about, hear, smell, or touch. For example: Take a healthy cooking class, join a gym, serving others in a physically demanding role or environment, sign up for a yoga class, learn or teach CPR, partake in a physically challenging missionary trip, see a championship sporting event, hear the roar of Niagara Falls, taste a fine wine, feel the warmth of a camp fire, savor the smell of a new car.

1) _____

2) _____

3) _____

#3 Health Concerns: Everybody knows you can pick your friends but you can't pick your family. Obviously, this means you can't avoid your family's medical history, or conditions passed on through their genes. Whether its high blood pressure, cholesterol, heart condition, cancer, weight, alcoholism, diabetes, etc., identify three health-related *concerns* that you need to stay on top of and combat with healthy habits and regular prayer.

1) _____

2) _____

3) _____

Living a rewarding retirement means being active and involved … knowing your health numbers … and taking care of your mental and spiritual well-being. Developing and maintaining a healthy retirement lifestyle contributes to your retirement identity, can help you stay socially involved, fill your time, stave off boredom, keep you from slipping into the dark side of retirement, and grow closer to God.

Remember, the real foundation for wealth is your complete and total health. Therefore, today's truly comprehensive retirement plan requires putting "how much you need to save" behind "the one who has saved you"

Personal Reflections & Retirement Applications

How would your retirement plans change if you were to lose one of your senses? Create a list of things you would like to see, hear, smell, taste, and touch. How does each sense plays a role in your spirituality?

SEE
- East Coast sunrise / West Coast sunset
- Broadway musical
- Arlington's Changing of The Guard
- _____
- _____
- _____

HEAR
- A baby's laugh
- Live performance of Beethoven Symphony #9
- Roar of Niagara Falls
- _____
- _____
- _____

TASTE
- Fresh squeezed OJ
- Chicago style pizza
- Fresh grilled bacon cheeseburger
- _____
- _____
- _____

TOUCH
- Silk bed sheets
- Snow ball
- Bubble wrap
- _____
- _____
- _____

SMELL
- New car
- Newborn baby
- Fresh cut grass
- _____
- _____
- _____

Chapter 7

RETIREMENT CONVERSATIONS

"Whoever of you loves life and desires to see many good days,
[13] keep your tongue from evil and your lips from telling lies."

Psalm 34:12-13 NIV

RETIREMENT CONVERSATIONS

*D*uring one of my workshops, a single woman shared with me that she was getting ready to retire and told a friend at work about her plans. Instead of a hug or simple congratulation, her friend replied "Well if you still want to meet or get together you'll have to make the arrangements and travel here to meet with me." I wasn't totally surprised by this response but many of you may be tempted to ask "what kind of friends does she have?"

In another workshop, a woman famously told her husband, "I married you for better or worse but not for lunch every day." Surprisingly, many couples are not on the same page when it comes to retirement, including whether or not they will eat every meal together or go separate ways on certain days and times.

Clean The Slate:

Forgiveness and relationship healing begins when you let go of your need to change the past. Realize that in order to rise up, advance, and become a more conscious person, you must be compassionate and forgiving towards yourself first.

Then, if you have any unresolved misunderstandings or resentments between you and a family member, friend, or co-worker make an effort to clean the slate and move forward instead of looking back.

Reality is, everyday life in retirement comes with its own stereotypes and assumptions. People may imagine how it's going to work, but aren't always effective in communicating those thoughts, which is exactly where danger lurks. If, for example, assumptions about how you'll spend your time, levels of family involvement, spiritual commitment, relationships needs, and household responsibilities aren't addressed before you retire, they can become points of contention and conflict throughout retirement.

Many of these potentially damaging assumptions and stereotypes can be resolved with proactive discussions about retirement before you actually retire. Investing the time to do so will establish an open and consistent approach to resolving issues and making decisions before they become a problem. The following questions about retirement can serve as topics of conversation to be discussed with family, friends, and colleagues. Use them to initiate conversations, gauge expectations, and to build a meaningful approach to your relationships in retirement.

Words are powerful, so be mindful of what you say and how you say it during these discussions. Differing views and opinions can intensify matters and make your time in retirement tense and emotionally draining. Therefore, be patient, and be sure to seek God before having any of these discussions.

"Know this, my beloved brothers: let every person be quick to hear, slow to speak, slow to anger"
James 1:19 ESV

"To answer before listening – that is folly and shame."
Proverbs 18:13 NIV

It's important to point out that you do not have to go through and answer every single question. The goal was to develop an extensive list that you could use to identify important topics as well as areas of retirement that you may not have thought about before.

At the end of the questions, there is a worksheet that allows you to organize your most important conversations, the people you need to have them with, and a time frame within which to have them. Whether, you're ten days or ten years away from retirement, start these conversations now instead of putting them off until later.

RETIREMENT CONVERSATIONS

Retirement Questions

What does your job provide that you will miss in retirement? Think about the mental, social, and physical aspects of your work. What steps can you take to maintain or replace them?

What skills and talents do you have and how do you plan to continue to use them?

Once you retire, you will no longer have a work identity. How will you identify yourself when you meet new people? When was the last time you were introduced to, or met, a retiree? What was your first impression of that person? How did they, in turn, refer to themselves?

What will you do with your time during retirement? How will the way you plan to spend time affect your relationships with others? What relationships may benefit; which ones, including previous work relationships, may need some preservation work? In your recent past, what jobs or leisure activities have you most enjoyed?

If you're married, will you go to bed and wake up at the same time? Will you eat breakfast, lunch, and dinner together every day? How much alone time will each of you need? What spiritual commitments will you seek together as well as independently?

What discussions should you begin having with your spouse, siblings, or your parents if you retire before they do? What impact is that likely to have on your relationship with them? What household expectations may change?

How will you relate to, and interact with, friends who are still working? To what degree would moving or spending time in a distant location affect family relationships and friendships?

How will your retirement affect family members? Will there be more or less visiting? What role will you play with your grandkids? Is everyone in agreement on this? How will you communicate your plans to your family?

What blessings do you need to count and thank God for? Do you have a spiritual plan? Will you set specific time(s) aside for worship including church attendance or Bible study?

RETIREMENT CONVERSATIONS

What temptations may pose the biggest threat to you and your family during retirement? What tools and resources are available to you in your area?

Are there some people in your life that drain you emotionally? People that you never seem to be able to please no matter what you do? Are there some boundaries you need to put in place to save your own sanity?

Which monthly bills and regular expenses will change? Will any expenses be eliminated; will any be added? How will healthcare costs figure into your retirement budget? Will you continue to save during retirement? What about tithing, giving to charity, or gifting to children or grandchildren?

What major expenses do you anticipate in retirement? Consider new vehicles, home updates, travel, helping out family or friends, etc.

Do family, friends, or Church anticipate an inheritance from your estate? What conflicts might arise among heirs? If you have a blended family, how will assets and possessions be used and divided? What personal and spiritual traditions do you want to pass on and be remembered for?

Are there any thoughts, questions, or concerns about retiring that keep you awake at night? Specifically, under what circumstances would you outlive your money? If you ran out of money, who would you ask for help?

Would the time, energy, or cost of supporting an adult child, grandchild, or parent have a bearing on your retirement budget or lifestyle? Are some family members more likely than others to ask for money, or move in with you? Have you established ground rules governing how you will help, or how modified living arrangements might work?

If you had to return to work, what kind of jobs would best utilize your strengths? What types of work would be most fulfilling?

RETIREMENT CONVERSATIONS

During retirement, which activities and people are likely to give you the best return on the time, energy, and the money you invest in them?

What role will your physical and mental health play during your retirement? Are you or your spouse putting your ideal retirement at risk because of an unhealthy habit or lifestyle? Do you anticipate that your current mental and physical health will impact your daily living, sex life, diet, and healthcare costs?

What is the one thing you hope no one finds out about your current retirement plan? What retirement conversations are you avoiding?

What conversations do you need to have with God? What worries, fears, hopes and dreams, do you need to hand over to Him? What are you asking God to do or help you with in retirement?

Retirement Conversations	Person(s)	Time Frame

By including God in your relationships and proactively discussing your thoughts and plans for everyday life in retirement you can avoid dangerous assumptions and living a less-than-meaningful retirement. Preemptive conversations strengthen not only your communication skills, but more importantly, the relationships that mean the most to you.

Since these issues are often overlooked and seldom planned for, don't be caught off guard if a family member, friend, or colleague seems confused about what retirement means to you. Be prepared to explain how you plan to spend your time in retirement, and make it clear that you're retiring from your job, not from life or your relationship with them.

Personal Reflections & Retirement Applications

_____

_____

_____

_____

_____

_____

_____

_____

_____

_____

_____

_____

_____

_____

_____

_____

_____

_____

_____

_____

_____

_____

_____

_____

_____

Chapter 8

CHRISTIAN RETIREMENT PLAN

"The LORD himself goes before you and will be with you; he will never leave you nor forsake you. Do not be afraid; do not be discouraged."

Deuteronomy 31:8 NIV

CHRISTIAN RETIREMENT PLAN

etirement Roots was created as a way to re-envision retirement as a spiritual journey by shining a light on salvation instead of personal savings. Many pre-retirees start out looking at retirement through a broken lens. A distorted view that tends to focus more on money than the individual. However, by going through the *Retirement Roots* worksheets, you have created a more personalized outlook through which you can see retirement for everything God has designed it to be.

Fact is, you've done some amazing work by completing the *Retirement Roots* exercises. The Retirement Perceptions quiz, for example, has turned your initial views and ideas about retirement into new realities … everyday realities with which you can seek God to help you to overcome stress and make the most of your newly discovered opportunities.

Salvation Prayer

Heavenly Father, I come to you in the name of Jesus and I admit that I am a sinner. I am sorry for my sins and the life that I have lived, and ask for your forgiveness. I believe that your son died on the cross for me, to save me, and I accept Jesus Christ as my own personal Savior.

I come to you now and ask you to take control of my life. Help me to live every day in a way that pleases you. I love you, Lord, and I thank you that I will spend all eternity with you.

You've uncovered your "Craft-matics" … the God-given things that make you feel happy and fulfilled each and every day. You have a list of things you're curious about, which will help you replace your work identity, fill your time, and overcome Satan's plan to tempt and disrupt your retirement plans and goals.

You have a list of friends to keep you happy, connected, and close to God… and finally, health goals that can not only help you walk off extra pounds or reduce stress, but also walk closer with our Lord and Savior. These are all vital ingredients to both a successful relationship with Christ and a successful retirement.

What I have learned over the years of helping clients prepare for every aspect of retirement is that it's empty! Meaning, God wants you to fill it up with things that will glorify Him. He wants us to be people who really love each other and care enough to be willing to pour hope, faith, and Jesus into their lives.

Retirement is also a blessing that many people never get to experience. It's not a time to be squandered or game in which to be a mere spectator. That means finding an end to selfish and harmful ways that draw us away from God. It's a time to build up that which enriches His Kingdom including making the most of your talents, relationships, body, mind, and spirit.

Finally, bear in mind that retirement is the final stage in life for which we can prepare ourselves for eternal life in heaven. A process that isn't automatic and doesn't just happen. It takes obedience, repentance, personal and financial sacrifice, prayer, faith, service to others, and acceptance of Jesus Christ as your Lord and Savior. If you haven't taken these steps before, but are ready to invite Jesus Christ into your life and heart, I offer you a salvation prayer in the sidebar on the left. By saying this prayer we believe you have been saved and born again. As a new Christian, talk to your small group leader, workshop leader, or seek out a Bible based church for next steps in your renewed life.

Your final *Retirement Roots* exercise is to crystallize your brand new thoughts, ideas, and beliefs by creating a one-page *Christian Retirement Plan*. This will become your personal reference point to seek God for guidance on the mental, social, physical, and spiritual areas of retirement. Each section will help you create a balanced approach to retirement with specific ideas for dealing with the many issues that are not addressed in traditional retirement planning.

1: Retirement Bumper Sticker
The first part of your final exercise is to create a retirement bumper sticker, or a mantra, that summarizes your new thoughts and feelings about retirement. Construct it using keywords, memorable phrase, or acronym that reflects something that stuck with you after completing one of the exercises. It might be something from your curious list, friends list, or simply a top-of-mind impression you have. For example, create a catchphrase such as *Free at last,* or *No more alarm clock.* Make it an acronym such as *NRR!* for *No Regrets Retirement*, or use your favorite Bible verse.

2: Things I Believe About Retirement
Next, imagine for a moment that you were asked to tell a room full of people what you believe about retirement. What would you say or compare it to? What does it offer you? Record 3-5 core beliefs in the space provided and use them in conversations to establish good expectations for what life in retirement means to you.

3: Top Five Curious List Items
Review your entire curious list and select your top five. List them in order of interest.

4: Retirement Conversations
Review your answers from the Retirement Conversations worksheet. Select the five most important conversations you need to have and list them here along with the target person to have the discussion with and timeframe for each conversation.

5: Wealth Concerns
While we didn't spend any time on the topic, there is the financial component to retirement that you need to consider. Take some time to write down any financial concerns you may have such as, How do I know if I can trust an advisor? Which pension option should I consider? Should I have gold and silver in my portfolio? Should I own bonds given the current interest rate environment and, if so, what kinds? What should I ask them, and how can I research them? Can I pay a professional to review my investments without being pressured to buy a product?

6: Health Habits, Opportunities, and Concerns
Similar to the top five curious list items, list 3-5 health habits, opportunities, or concerns that you want to address immediately.

7: Spiritual Action Plan
Retirement isn't the end or the ultimate prize. Getting into heaven is. Take a moment to listen to what God has placed on your heart and in your mind. Then write down three to five real and lasting commitments you will take to start storing up treasures for heaven. Whatever the decision, use this section of the plan to start creating a more meaningful retirement right now.

> *"What good is it for someone to gain the whole world, yet forfeit their soul?"*
> *Mark 8:36 NIV*

CHRISTIAN RETIREMENT PLAN

1. Retirement Bumper Sticker

_____
_____
_____

2. What I Believe About Retirement

1) _____
2) _____
3) _____
4) _____
5) _____

3. Top Five Curious List Items

1) _____
2) _____
3) _____
4) _____
5) _____

4. Retirement Conversations	Person(s)	Time Frame
_____	_____	_____
_____	_____	_____
_____	_____	_____
_____	_____	_____
_____	_____	_____

5. Wealth Concerns & Opportunities

1) _____   2) _____   3) _____

6. Health Habits, Opportunities, and Issues

1) _____
2) _____
3) _____
4) _____
5) _____

7. Spiritual Action Plan

1) _____
2) _____
3) _____
4) _____
5) _____

CHRISTIAN RETIREMENT PLAN

Hang your completed list where you will see it every day. Use it to stay conscious of the fact that money can't buy great friends, good health, or a ticket to heaven, but a little planning, faith, and commitment to our Lord and Savior can help you make it everlasting.

God bless you and thank you for completing *Retirement Roots* and placing your trust in God and the program. I hope your thoughts and plans about retirement have been dramatically transformed and that the work you've done helps you realize, the best is yet to come!

Personal Reflections & Retirement Applications

_____

_____

_____

_____

_____

_____

_____

_____

_____

_____

_____

_____

_____

_____

_____

_____

_____

_____

_____

_____

_____

_____

_____

Sources

Source Information

Chapter 2: Retirement Perceptions
Retirement study: Forbes.com, Can Your Marriage Survive Retirement, by Robert Laura, quoting Rob Pascale PhD, January 2013

Chapter 3: Retirement Dark Side
Chilling RX: The New York Times; "Addicts of A Certain Age: Baby Boomers Need Help." March 6, 2008.

Chapter 4: Retirement Foundations:
Adapted from George Kinder, <u>Seven Stages of Money Maturity</u>, Dell Publishing, a division of Random House, copyright 1999, p.154.156, 158.

Chapter 4: Retirement Foundations:
Rick Warren: Forbes.com, Pastor Rick Warren Is Well prepared For A Purpose Driven Retirement, by Robert Laura, March 2013

Chapter 5: Retirement Curious &Friend Lists
Harvard Study, The Five Essential Elements by Tom Rath, Jim Harter, P.17Gallup press, 2010, Adapted from Clark, et, al, The Economic Journal, June 2008

Chapter 5: Retirement Curious &Friend Lists
Communication Research: Forbes.com, interview with Rob Pascale PhD, January 2013.

Robert Laura

is a pioneer in the psychology and social science of retirement planning and is a highly sought after presenter at retirement conferences and meetings across the country. He is a three-time best-selling author and nationally syndicated columnist for Forbes.com, Financial Advisor Magazine, and NextAvenue.org. His work has reached millions of retirement readers through seven books, twelve guides, and over 800 articles. In addition to his own writings, he frequently appears in major business media outlets such as the Wall Street Journal, USA Today, CNBC, MarketWatch, Investor's Business Daily, New York Times, and more.

As a former social worker turned money manager and author, he has found that retirement is among the most fascinating, yet least understood, phases of life. As a result, he has developed a powerful message to tackle the mental, social, spiritual, and financial aspects of retirement. All of his work reflects his ground-breaking efforts to challenge the status quo of traditional retirement planning and help people create a No-Regrets Retirement Plan!

Robert has been a speaking and teaching financial and non-financial retirement based programs for over 20 years. His presentations are ideal for every group, from business owners and executives to employees, associations, and retirees.

His conversational and humorous style allows his audiences to get educated in an entertaining way as he creates a memorable experience that touches both the mind and heart. With thought-provoking insights, vivid stories, and a frequent dose of humor, he reaches audiences in a way they do not forget.

Robert has garnered a unique look at wealth and retirement by not only working closely with his own clients for the last twenty years, but also by interviewing numerous celebrities, entertainers, and athletes including Pastor Rick Warren, Deion Sanders, John Sally, Gymnast Shannon Miller, Golfer Annika Sorenstam, Singer Amy Grant, HGTV's the Property Brothers, Pawn Star Rick Harrison, Cheech & Chong, Impersonator Rich Little and more.

He is the founder of the Wealth & Wellness Group, Certified Professional Retirement Coach Designation, and RetirementProject.org. He holds several designations including Certified Kingdom Advisor, Accredited Asset Management Specialist, Certified Mutual Fund Counselor, Chartered Retirement Planning Counselor, and Certified Retirement Coach.

He also serves as an expert witness and consultant to attorneys, providing courtroom testimony and litigation support on investment matters.

Robert is married to his amazing wife Amie and together they have a blended family of four wonderful children. Connor, Ava, Luke, and Drake.

Best-selling Author
rl.robertlaura@gmail.com